THE

DAYSMAN

AND

OTHER WORKS

BY
BISHOP K. C. PILLAI
OF INDIA

The scriptures used throughout this book are quoted from the King James Version unless otherwise noted.

While limited grammatical editing has been done to enhance contemporary readability, care has been taken to preserve the integrity of Pillai's work.

To ensure the most optimal reading experience, the highest standards of quality control are used. Protocols such as optical character recognition (OCR) scans and double proofing are used to eliminate errors. These protocols ensure cleaner, more readable books.

ISBN 978-1-948987-04-2

BISHOP K. C. PILLAI OF INDIA

ORIGINALLY PUBLISHED BY
INTER-FAITH BIBLE SEMINAR
EAST STANWOOD, WASHINGTON

AS

"LIGHT THROUGH AN EASTERN WINDOW"

CONTENTS

FOREWORD

This booklet has been reproduced to preserve and make available the teachings and knowledge by Bishop K.C. Pillai of Eastern manners and customs. Originally printed by those who studied and learned from him, this booklet was part of Bishop Pillai's many outreach settings that he often regarded as: "Light through an Eastern Window."

As a convert to Christianity from Hinduism, Bishop Karnam Chengalvaraya Pillai, D.D. came to the Western world on a singular mission: to teach the Eastern culture of the Bible. Although Christianity is generally considered a Western religion, it is important to recognize that the Bible itself was written and set in the Eastern world, and it must be viewed through the light of that Eastern window. It is primarily the area referred to at varying times as the Near East, Middle East, or Orient where the people and events described in the Bible resided. Resultantly, in order to really understand the Bible, one must become knowledgeable of the culture, manners, and customs of the Eastern world.

While understanding cultural differences is important in many aspects of life, it is most significant in the field of Biblical research. As Bishop Pillai shared:

> When we consider the "light through an Eastern window" we must always remember that the Bible is an Eastern book, written by men who spoke an Eastern language and used words expressing Eastern customs. Many of the Eastern phrases used as figures of speech are interpreted literally in the West and

that to our own hurt. Doing this has caused great confusion and much harm to the work of God.

The Bible is filled with passages that perplex the Westerner's mind, simply because he lacks an understanding of the peculiar idioms, traditions, customs, and manners underlying the scriptural passage. Those same Scriptures, however, were readily understood by the people that inhabited the Bible lands when they were first written. And, since a great deal of those expressions and practices remained unchanged in the Orient even to modern times, present-day Easterners often grasp the meaning of Scriptures that elude Christians in the Western world.

Born in 1902, at the time of K. C. Pillai's early life, his native India had remained an isolated country for thousands of years. Therefore, the customs and manners of the people were still aligned with the Eastern, Biblical culture; and as such, it provided an indispensable resource.

K.C. Pillai held a doctorate of Divinity and served as Bishop of the Indian Eastern Orthodox Church, Antiochean Succession in North Madras. In the United States, he held the offices of Primate of the American Episcopal Church in Birmingham, Alabama; and Archbishop of the Indian Eastern Orthodox Church. First introduced to the United States by Dr. H.J. Ironside, then pastor of the Moody Church, Pillai gained acclaim throughout America as the foremost authority on the Eastern culture of the Bible. He describes how he came to teach Orientalisms to the Western world.

> I have been asked to state how it was that I came to teach the Orientalisms of the Bible. I suppose it seemed like an accident at the time, but of course with God, nothing is an accident.

> I am an Indian by birth, of the Hindu caste, and of

the Christian religion. I was converted to Christianity in my own village in the south of India, but it was not until I went to England for the first time, in 1932, that I became aware of the great need for the Westerners to understand the culture of the East so that they could better understand the Bible.

When I went to churches in England, I heard preachers who simply did not understand what they were trying to preach, and in fact had missed some great Biblical truths due to ignorance of the Oriental idioms, customs, parables, and the like. I began to enlighten them on these matters. Later, my church, the Eastern Orthodox Church, assigned me to the ministry of teaching these things in the Western world. This I have done, both on the continent of Europe, in the British Isles, and now on the North American continent. As far as I know, I am the only Hindu convert to Christianity who has engaged in this kind of teaching.

For over twenty-five years I have continued this work under the title, "Light through an Eastern Window"; I have been in churches of nearly every denomination and also in colleges and seminaries.

In the summer of 1953, the Bishop met Dr. Victor Paul Wierwille, a man who was to have a profound impact on his life and understanding of the Bible. For many years, Dr. Wierwille, a graduate of Princeton Theological Seminary, quested for greater understanding of the Bible. His tremendous spiritual hunger led him to travel throughout the country in order to learn from various Christian leaders, as well as inviting them to Ohio to share their knowledge with his rapidly growing ministry. V.P. Wierwille's invitation to Pillai for a brief visit that summer led to an extended visit a couple of months later. Over the course of six weeks, the two men read every verse in the Bible together, with the Bishop pointing out and explaining each Orientalism that appeared.

The relationship between V.P. Wierwille and K.C. Pillai proved mutually beneficial in many ways. As told in the book *Born Again to Serve*, Dr. Wierwille expressed his admiration for Bishop Pillai. "I'll always be grateful for that man. There was much in the Bible I couldn't understand and didn't know. I had no idea about Eastern culture. But the Bishop did; and when he explained Eastern culture to me, it became simple. An interesting thing about our relationship was that the Bishop taught me Eastern customs, and I taught him renewed mind, of which he became the greatest exponent." Later the Bishop said, "I came over 10,000 miles from India to the United States just to hear the truth from Dr. Wierwille."

Bishop Pillai continued working closely with Dr. Wierwille for the remainder of his life. His articles explaining Eastern manners and customs of the Bible, "Light through an Eastern Window," appeared regularly in the Biblical research magazine Dr. Wierwille's ministry published. He taught fellowships, classes, and camps alongside Dr. Wierwille. He continued illuminating the Western world with his knowledge of the Orientalisms found in the Bible until the time of his death on February 10, 1970.

The interest Bishop Pillai generated in the field has led to numerous further studies by other scholars in the field of manners and customs in the Bible, as well. His books and teachings continue to illuminate and inspire students of the Bible throughout the world. Bishop Pillai's work was published in three books during his lifetime: *Light through an Eastern Window; Orientalisms of the Bible, Volume 1*; and *Orientalisms of the Bible Volume 2*. While those books remain a valuable resource, the small volumes represent only a fraction of Bishop Pillai's work in the field of manners and customs of the Bible.

Bishop K.C. Pillai left a rich legacy of work that far exceeds those three books. Volumes of Pillai's Eastern studies exist in both written and audio recordings. This booklet is one that has been restored to open the doors of enlightenment into the culture that provides the setting for the lives, events, and tenets central to Christianity. Knowledge of the Eastern customs and idioms used in the Scriptures is essential to understanding the Bible.

ETERNALLY BLESSED EDITORIAL STAFF

*   *   *   *   *   *

God sends us His blessings in many disguises. He sent Bishop K. C. Pillai, a servant of Christ, from India to East Stanwood, Washington, to touch our lives. For one month, he lectured here five hours daily, expounding the Scriptures in the light of the culture and people of the East. All who heard him were blessed, but for some of us, the course of our lives was abruptly changed.

It is our prayer that this little booklet, containing four of these lectures, will prove a blessing, both by a richer understanding of the Word of God, and by souls finding Christ as Saviour.

Bishop Pillai's stay in East Stanwood, and the publication of these lectures was sponsored by a small group of Christian business men, who feel that to God belongs all the praise and glory for any good resulting from this work.

INTER-FAITH BIBLE SEMINAR

THE DAYSMAN

Tonight let us turn to the book of Job, chapter 9, verses 32 and 33. While you are looking up these verses, I would like to give you a little account of their background. There was a man named Job, who was a perfect and upright man before God. God himself said that he was a perfect and upright man. But one day Satan came to God concerning Job, and said, ". . .thou hast blessed the work of his hands, and his substance is increased in the land. But put forth thine hand now, and touch all that he hath, and he will curse thee to thy face." Then God said to Satan, "Behold, all that he hath is in thy power; only upon himself put not forth thine hand." Thus God gave Satan permission to go and try Job. Thus God permitted Satan to take away all that Job had—his sons, his daughters, his sheep, his cattle, his oxen—everything that he had was taken away. One after another, one after another, they were taken away from Job without any fault on his part. Often when we lose something, we begin to grumble and complain and say, "I've been a good man; I never did anybody any harm; if there is a God at all, why should I suffer the loss of these things?"

The moment we lose something, most of us immediately begin to grumble and complain against God. Job could have made an argument with God. He could have said, "Lord, look here. You said I am a perfect and an upright man, without any fault in thy sight at all. Yet you have taken away all that I had, except my wife, and she is just an old grumbler and no help to me at all." When Job was afflicted, his wife came to him and said, "Curse God, and die." Today, in the midst of seeming

13

crisis, similar to the one that Job faced, we all know that some wives do speak in the same grumbling way. That is why Christian men should marry only Christian women, and Christian women should marry only Christian men, because if a husband loses something, a Christian wife will not carry on and nag her husband, or hinder him, or become an additional burden. But Job's wife was a grumbler, . . . "Curse God, and die," she said. "Thou speakest as one of the foolish women speakest," Job said to the woman. "What? Shall we receive good at the hand of God, and shall we not receive evil? The Lord gave, and the Lord hath taken away, blessed be the name of the Lord."

When you feel that you have cause to grumble and complain and want to fret and fume and accuse God and everyone else, then praise God! When God took away all those things from Job, Job praised God, and said, "The Lord gave, and the Lord hath taken away; blessed be the name of the Lord." The next time anything seemingly wrong happens to you or to me, let us praise God, instead of complaining, and see what a marvelous thing will happen to us. That seemingly evil thing will turn out to be a mighty blessing. I was very sorry today as I passed through your town of East Stanwood, to see a store that had just burned down. I do not know the gentlemen who owned the store at all, but seeing this grocery store and hardware store and butcher shop burned has hurt me very much in my heart and in my mind, and made me very restless. My dear brother who owned that store, if you are here, if you are a child of God, don't complain, but praise God! You see, God can give you a building ten times as good. He can give you a better business—yes, a hundred-fold better business, than the one you have lost. "All things work together for good to them that love God." Whenever any believer loses anything, even though it may seem hard to bear, he should begin to praise God, knowing and believing that all things will work together for good. Then you will never have a complaint, because you are praising God. Then God will make all things beautiful and good—a hundred-fold better than it would have been had you complained.

So Job was that kind of a man! A little later he said, "Though he slay me, yet will I trust in him." When he had sores all over his body, and when he was rubbing those sores with the potsherd as he sat in the ashes and dust, he could still say, "Though he slay me, yet will I trust in him." Poor old Job! He had lost all his sons and daughters, all his sheep and all his property—he had lost everything except his wife, and now he had a tremendous disease with sores all over his body and sat in dust and ashes. Do you understand the meaning of dust and ashes?

In the East, we sit in the dust and throw ashes all over the body to show the greatest humility possible. It is a manifestation of the greatest humility to sit in the dust. We say, "Lord, I came from the dust, to the dust I return. I would return alive to the dust." That's the true meaning of sitting in dust and ashes. "All shall return to the dust again in death, but now, Lord, I return to the dust alive, in order to show my humility and repentance." That's what we say, and that's what sitting in the dust means.

Now what do ashes mean? Ashes are symbolic of salvation to the non-Christian gentiles—symbolic of salvation by sacrifice. Ashes are symbolic of sacrifice, because you remember that they killed and burned a red heifer and made ashes of it. The non-Christian gentile puts dust and ashes all over his body and on his forehead meaning, "Lord, please save me on the merit of these ashes—on the merit of this sacrifice, of which the ashes are symbolic." If any Hindu puts ashes on his forehead in the morning before breakfast, that means he is saying to God, "Lord, not on my merit, but on the merits of the sacrifice which is represented in the ashes —on the merit of the ashes, Lord, please forgive my sin. I will be protected, Lord, through this day on the merits of the ashes which I have on my forehead, which are the symbol of salvation by sacrifice." Ashes were put on the forehead in this way long before Christianity came into being.

The Hindus believe that ashes are symbolic of sacrifice —that's why most Hindus sit in dust and ashes and repent. "I am covered with the blood," the Christians say. The Hindus say, "I am covered with ashes." To the Hindu, ashes have the same meaning as the blood of Jesus Christ has to us. That's why, if a man has ashes all over his forehead, he's not a dirty man; he's as clean as any man that you could ever find anywhere in any other country. He has bathed, but he has put ashes on his forehead. To any Westerner, who is ignorant of the ways of the East, he thinks that this man is a dirty man, because he has ashes on his forehead. You see how mixed up people can get about some of the customs of the East?

The Hindu also puts a little bit of ashes or dust on his lips and on his tongue. That means, "Not only do I put ashes on my body as a sort of protection, but I also put my insides under the protection of God by putting a little bit of ashes in my mouth." That's why David said, "I've eaten ashes like bread." Look this up in Psalm 102:9, where it says, "For I have eaten ashes like bread, and mingled my drink with weeping." What a wonderful statement that is! "I've eaten ashes like bread," means, "Lord, I've continually protected myself inside and out-side with the ashes, which are symbolic of salvation." "Mingled my drink with weeping," means, "Lord, I have wept so continuously, that the tears have dropped into the water that I was drinking." These are symbolic East-ern expressions that have a deeper meaning than you can explain in the English language. I wish I were speaking in my own language tonight, so I could give you the true picture of the ashes, but I have done the best that I could for you in the English language.

So Job sat down in the ashes, and he was satisfied. Now what is sackcloth, and what is its meaning? Sack-cloth is a coarse material made of camel's hair or goat's hair and is worn as a sign of mourning. Instead of a smooth cloth, made of good material, we wear a course material made of camel's hair. We wear this sackcloth when we fast, in order to manifest to God, that instead of the good silk clothing, we wear this coarse clothing that will hurt the body. Clothes made of camel's hair or goat's hair feels like pins pricking the skin. "So Lord, instead of being comfortable when I pray to you, I am crushing the body by wearing clothes made of camel's hair or goat's hair." So that's what sackcloth, ashes and dust symbolize. When you go inside a Roman Catholic church, you will see that they have the holy water and the ashes, also. They put a little bit in their mouths, for the same reason as the Hindus, as you who have been Roman Catholics know.

Of course, that custom has come here from India, from the Hindu people, because Christianity is only two thou-sand years old, and the Hindu religion is thousands of years old. India has been giving these things to other nations for generations, but that doesn't make India any better than any other country. India is just as much of a sinner as America is, if not worse, because every Hindu that has sinned in India must sit in dust and ashes, and pray and fast and mourn with sackcloth. They will never find peace with God unless they forsake the man-made systems and look to Jesus. This is my stand, which I make concerning all the nations of the world. It is not by might, nor by power; it is not by ashes, nor by sackcloth; it is not by fasting, nor by praying; but by faith in the works of Christ alone, by which man can be saved and find the peace of God.

So Job sat down in dust and ashes and said, "Naked came I out of my mother's womb, and naked shall I return thither: the Lord gave, and the Lord hath taken away; blessed be the name of the Lord." Job believed that what he had lost was from God in the first place. He believed, too, that it was by the permission of God that he had lost these things, because when God gives us these things, he has the right to take them away again. When he has the right to take them away, he has the right, also, to give them back to us again, if we will only keep our eyes upon God, from whom all blessings come. That's what Job believed. He was able to praise God when he had a legitimate reason to curse God for all the things he had lost.

His friends came to see him by and by—you know how that goes? If you lose anything, or get into trouble, your friends come along to try to comfort you. You know what your friends really do, don't you? Well, most of your friends usually try to frighten you! Go to your friends when you are in trouble, and see how they frighten you. They mean well, but they'll frighten you just the same. So Job's friends said to him, "Poor Job! Look here —I thought so, Job. You were a religious man, weren't you? Well, after all your being religious, Job, look how you lost all those things. I don't think God had any part in it. I think there is something wrong with you, Job. In fact, we have always thought that there was something wrong, Job!" That's the way friends talk, you know. "I thought so, I thought so," they'll tell you, but they didn't think that at all—they are only saying that they did. So don't go to your friends with your troubles.

Long before I took up my ministry in India, I had a little boil here on my thumb. It was just a scratch here that got infected, and I put something on my thumb to tie it up. So I was writing in my office, keeping my thumb up so it wouldn't hang down and pain so much, when one of the other 65 men working in the office saw my bandaged thumb and came over to me and said, "Hey, what's wrong with you?" "Oh, it's not much, just a little sore," I said. "No, no, don't be a fool! Put your pen down and open up the bandage and let me see it. You know there is a disease going around in the city, don't you? You have not heard about it? You have not read about it in the papers? It begins just like this, then it becomes big, then it goes to every joint and to the brain, and when it gets there, it bursts, and you are dead!" You know what I did? I let him open up the bandage. "Oh, dear, dear, you must take care of this. . . !" And his eyes opened big, big, big—and the more wide his eyes opened, the more fearful I became. So I asked my boss for a day off, and went back home and lay on the bed like a fool. That's all there was to it, nothing more happened. You see, I had become nervous by my friend's talk. So when you are in trouble, if you can't go to God with your trouble, don't go to any human, unless you know that he is a man of God.

I remember that after I was saved, not only did my father and mother get rid of me by burying my picture, but my society, my caste, put sanctions upon my relations' households. I have hundreds of relatives in India, but my father and mother and my three sisters are now dead. I still have uncles, aunts, cousins and many other relatives living there. So they put sanctions on my relatives and said, "Don't talk to this man's mother or father, or his uncles or aunts, or his sisters, because their son became a Christian." Thus the whole family was ostracized, because I became a Christian. I was studying in a seminary then, a hundred miles from home, and my uncle came up to talk to me. He called me out from a big meeting to talk with me and said, "You know, we got rid of you, and got you away from us because we were afraid of sanctions, but now we can't get water from the well, the baker won't sell us bread, the grocer won't sell us groceries. The sanctions have been put upon us because of you. What shall we do now?" So I went to a group of three of my Christian friends whom I thought could give me a solution, and told them what was happening to my people. "Well, we can't help those things. Those things will be so. Worse things might come yet," they said. They did not offer me any help at all, they only made things worse. What do you think they should have told me? Well, they should have told me, "Praise God. God is able to save you and your people!" That's what they should have told me. They should have said to me, "Take your problems to the Lord, because the Lord is able. Don't get frightened—it is only a bluff to get you frightened. Our God is able—He is high above all!" But they did not speak that way. That is why I have given up going to human beings when I am in trouble. When everything is going well, then I go to my friends, but not when I am in trouble, because then they only frighten me.

So Job was content to sit in dust and ashes, and said, "Though he slay me, yet will I trust in him," but at this point, Job's friends came to him. These friends talked to him like you would have talked. They are called, "Job's Comforters," but they were not comforters at all! They were very sincere men, but they looked only upon the surface of things. When we get in trouble, we are all inclined to come to a judgment by looking at the surface of things. Our friends are all like that, too, they only look on the surface of things. We should not judge on the surface of things, but we should judge righteous judgment. Jesus said, "Judge not according to the appearance, but judge righteous judgment." (John 7:24). Don't get fooled and baffled by looking at the surface of things, but look away from the surface, down deep at the truth, because righteous judgments are based on the truth.

Don't base your judgment on facts, because facts change, but truth does not change. Facts may be so today, but not so tomorrow. It may be a fact, but it's not the truth. Truth never changes, but facts do change. So your trouble may be very real and be a fact—you may have trouble today, but tomorrow your trouble may be gone, and the facts have changed. But the truth, which is Jesus, never changes and is always peace; truth is always joy; truth is always liberty; truth is always gladness; truth is always success; truth is always victory—therefore Jesus said, "Judge not according to the appearance, but judge righteous judgment." This means that you should base your judgment on the truth, which does not alter.

Many of you say, "Oh, but that's a fact!" It may be a fact for you, but it is not the truth, because it does not stay the same. Truth is always the same! You should look to truth when you go to work in the morning, and upon arrival find that you are fired. When you get fired, you do not have any more money coming in and your wife begins to nag—of course she will begin to nag, because she wonders how she is going to pay the rent. Her eyes are on the rent, that's why she worries. When you get fired, the facts are that you do not have any more money coming in to pay the rent and the other bills—and these are facts, but it is not the truth. The truth is that, "My God shall supply all your need according to his riches in glory by Christ Jesus." (Philippians 4:19). That's the truth! The fact is that you got fired, but you may get a better job tomorrow, because facts change. Therefore, Jesus says for us not to judge according to the appearance, but to judge righteous judgment, which is the best judgment, based on the truth. This type of judgment is always victorious, it is always glorious, it is always successful.

Job believed in judging righteous judgment, but his friends said, "You lost all your sons, you lost all your daughters, you lost all your sheep, you lost all your camels and you have never harmed anybody. If there is a God at all, why should you lose everything at once? There may be a God if he would take all your possessions a little at a time—but to take everything at once— well, we don't think there is a God at all! Poor old Job, all the people thought that you were a religious man, but we always thought that there was something wrong with you!" "We don't think so,"—"We thought so," is what our friends always say. People like Job's comforters will always tell you something negative—something that will make things look worse than they actually are.

Now turn with me to the book of Job, chapter 9, verses 32 and 33, where Job is talking about God, when he says, "For He is not a man, as I am, that I should answer Him, and we should come together in judgment." In effect, Job was saying to his friends, "Look here, my friends, it was God that allowed me to lose those things which I lost. And God is not a man, as I am, that we should come together in judgment. If God were a man, I could take Him before the judgment seat and ask the judges to ask God why He let me suffer these things; but God is not a man, as I am, that we should come together in judgment."

Now verse 33 says, "Neither is there any daysman betwixt us, that might lay his hand upon us both." In that part of the East that we are talking about, which is India, Palestine and Egypt, there are three systems of law, or government. There is the law or government by the elders of the gate; there is the daysman; and there is the civil court. Government by the elders of the gate is an old type of democracy—you read about it in the Bible. In every town in the East there are the elders of the gate, maybe twenty or thirty of them, chosen by the people once a year. They are elected by the people, for the people, and are the government of the people. This system is as old as the hills. In America, government of the people, by the people, for the people may be a new thing, but not so in the East, nor in the scriptures. The elders of the gate, therefore, is one system of government.

Another system of government is the civil court, or police court, or county court, or the magistrate's court —or whatever name this court has in that particular country. In India, this court used to be the British court, whose judges were appointed by the British government. The elders of the gate and the police courts handle cases about the same way, and do about the same job. If a man has quarreled with his wife, or his wife with him, both of them are brought before the elders of the gate for judgment. The elders of the gate sit at the gate of the city for two hours every morning to judge all the cases brought in to them. They judge all the little local crimes. If a man owed money and didn't pay, he is brought before the elders of the gate and they pass judgment. "Hey, look here," they say, "You go and pay your debts. If you don't pay, we'll give your cow or oxen to the man to whom you owe the money."

If some of the boys of the town are naughty, they'll bring the boys and their parents before them. "Look here," the elders of the gate tell the parents, "If you don't look after your children and make them civilized, we shall ostracize you. Don't let your children run wild in the street, but get them to bed by 8 o'clock. If your children continue running wild, we are going to punish you, because you are bringing a disgrace on our society." That's the way we correct our society—a person can't go wrong very long in the East without being found out, and immediately, that person is brought before the elders of the gate for judgment. When they punish a person, and that person has to post a fine, the money goes to charity, to hospitals, and to the community.

The police court, appointed by the city, does about the same type of thing in its judgments. If a man is drunk, the police bring him before the judge, and the judge gives him six months or a $50.00 fine. If he goes bad and gets drunk again, the judge gives him 3 months and a $40.00 fine—that's the way these courts go on. So both the police courts and the elders of the gate do the same thing—they punish the wrong-doer by the witness of two or three people. But punishing the wrong-doer does not heal the wound on the inside. Jail never cured anyone. If you put a man in jail, when he gets out, he does a worse thing. So, because punishing the wrong-doer does not heal the wound on the inside, the religious people of the East will not go to the elders of the gate or to the police courts with their troubles. The people who are religious go to the daysman to settle their disputes.

What is a daysman? Who is he? How does he spring up? I will answer these questions for you. The daysman is not nominated or elected. He is not appointed like the judges are. Every town has a daysman, and in a town like East Stanwood, a man springs up by his dignity, his divinity, his good character and by his education. A man comes up that way and becomes a leader for the whole town, because of the sheer respect of the people given to him. His object is to see that all the people of the town live in peace. The people of the West have been told that the word "daysman" means "umpire." But the word "daysman" does not mean "umpire!" An umpire is a man that stands in a baseball field and says, "You're right, he's wrong." An umpire does not have to have much sense, and because of this fact, there is as much difference between a daysman and an umpire as there is between cheese and chalk.

The word for daysman in some of the languages of the East means "great soul." In India, the word "Mahatma" means great soul, and it is the name given to Gandhi—he was called Mahatma Gandhi; a great soul. A daysman is a very highly respected man, a highly honored man, and generally a wealthy man, who does not have to work for a living. If he is wealthy, he has plenty of time to give to being a daysman, and he sees to it that there are no quarrels or fighting, no gossiping, no backbiting, or no character slaughter among the people. He sees to it that everyone lives in peace and quietness.

Many people say something like this, "That man smokes and drinks and curses, so he must be a bad man!" Now look here, believers do worse sins and crimes than smoking and drinking, do you know that? Believers will assassinate the character of people—they will say something like this, "There is nothing wrong with Mr. Smith, BUT—," and just leave the sentence hanging there on the word "but." In so doing, they have assassinated Mr. Smith's character. We may not drink, smoke or curse, but we do worse when we assassinate the character of a person.

An assassination of the character of a person, whether that person is good or bad is a terrible wrong, even though the facts that are stated are correct. Even though what you say may be correct, you are still wrong. We don't realize this great truth, and I don't think that you grasp it now. Even though the facts that you speak about a man are correct, you are still wrong in the sight of God, because you grieve yourself by speaking evil against your brother. You not only are harming the person against whom you are speaking, but you are also harming yourself, because anything negative "sucks your blood" and hurts your spirit and your personality! Our mighty Lord Jesus told us these truths for our own interest.

So this daysman sees to it that we all live together in peace. Let us take an example—three men living in the same community have some problem or legal issue between them. One of the men says to the others, "My dear brothers, we are all Hindu religious people, aren't we? We should be ashamed to go to the police courts or to the elders of the gate; aren't we able to judge ourselves?" So they take their problem to the daysman, who helps them settle their issue. The Hindus are taught that if they cannot settle a question among themselves, they should go to the daysman, and not to the elders of the gate or to the police court. Saint Paul said, in 1 Corinthians 6:1 to 5: "Dare any of you, having a matter against another, go to law before the unjust, and not before the saints?—Know ye not that we shall judge angels?—Is it so, that there is not a wise man among you?"

I will give you another example, so that you may see how the daysman handles situations that arise. Suppose that Brother Jacobson here, and myself are boys, say 18 or 19 years old, living in India or Palestine, and we both are religious people. We might be Hindu, or Mohammedan, or Christian—what religion does not matter. Suppose we had an issue between us—suppose that I had borrowed some money from Brother Jacobson, and had not paid it back. Each time that he had asked me for the money I would say, "I'll pay, I'll pay," but I never had paid. Then one day when he asked me for the money, and when I didn't pay, he got angry and hit me.

When my father and his father heard about it that night, they knew that we were in hot water, because they were religious people, and they knew that they must solve this problem correctly. If they locked their boys up, that wouldn't solve the problem, because punishing does not heal the wounds, it only causes bitterness. So my father and Brother Jacobson's father tell us, "You are very naughty boys. You will have to look at each other's faces every morning for the rest of your lives. You should have love for each other. The jail or the police court will not solve this thing; neither will going to the elders of the gate. We want you boys to heal your wounds of all bitterness—let's go to the daysman!"

So our parents grab us and take us to the daysman. We go to his house and knock on the door and he says, "Come in." He is a very beloved and honorable person of that town. We go in and he asks, "Wouldn't you like something to drink this morning?" And then he calls for coconut milk the first thing. He doesn't ask who you are, or whether you belong to the same religion that he does, or whether you belong to the same church that he does, or any of that. We walk in as human beings; and as a person, he respects you as a brother, "Come in," he says, and gets you a drink, and doesn't even ask you your name. He doesn't say, "Can I do anything for you?" Neither does he peek through a small window, as they do in England to see who it is, before opening the door. "Come in," the daysman calls to whoever is knocking at his door—so we drink something and then sit down, and the daysman waits until you tell him why you are there.

So my father gets up and says, "Mahatmaji, (you should always put "ji" after a man's name in India—if he is your pastor, you say "Pastorji"), this boy is my son." And if all the parties in the room are Hindus, the father will place his three fingers on his forehead and make a small bow. This is done only when one Hindu meets another, and means that "God and you and I are one." Jesus said, "I and the Father are one," and this same

idea has run through the Eastern philosophy for thousands
of years. Both parents in turn will say to the daysman,
"This boy is my son." Then they will say, "Our sons
had a quarrel and we want you to settle it for them. We
don't want to go to court, because the court won't heal
the wounds. We want the boys to love each other, so we
brought them to you."

"Oh, is that so? I see. Come on boys, what are your
names?" Suppose I say my name is John, and suppose
Brother Jacobson says his name is Jim. "Come on,
Johnny, sit down here," he'll say to me. He will sit in
the middle and put his hands upon the shoulders of both
of the boys. The boy that did the wrong, Jimmy, the one
who beat me up because I owed him the money, he'll
put on his right hand side. The guilty person is always
placed on the right hand side, because he loves him the
most. The other person is always put on the left hand
side. Then the daysman actually puts his arms around us
both, to show his affection for both of us. "Now, Jimmy,"
he'll say to Jacobson, "What did you do?"

"Well," Jimmy will reply, "Johnny owed me money
and he never paid, and never paid, and never paid, until
I got wild and punched him in the nose." Now, if we
are Hindus, the daysman will get out the Hindu bible,
the Veda; if we are Mohammedans, he will get out the
Mohammedan bible, the Koran; or if we are Christians,
he will get out the Bible. He has all these books, and
will get out the book that fits each group's religion. So,
as we are Hindus, he will take out the Veda, open it up,
and say, "Ah, you punched his nose—do you know that
he is your brother?"

"Yes sir."

"And you know that if God had punched you in the
nose for all the things that you have done wrong since
you were small, you wouldn't have any nose left, would

you? When you lend to your brother, you must not expect it back," the daysman tells Jimmy. The Hindu and the Jewish religions both teach that if you find a poor brother within your gates and you lend to him, you must not expect it back, unless he comes to pay it back to you. So you lose that money? Well, if your brother does not come to pay you, do not ask for it.

Thus the daysman talks to Jimmy, showing him the scripture, convicting him, and proving to him that he is wrong. He takes all the time needed, two or three hours or more, if necessary, to show him that he is in the wrong. He will say, "When you lent him the money, you gave it to him. If he is not able to pay, you should not have asked him. You broke one law there, asking him for it. Then you broke another law by hitting him. And then what you lent him was not your money, it was God's money—it belonged to God."

The Bible teaches that, too, that what you have is not your own. If God had not given you the strength to earn, how could you have earned your money? God gave you the power to earn, so that you may lend the money to a brother! The Bible teaches that whosoever will give a cup of cold water in the name of the Lord shall be blessed. "For whosoever shall give you a cup of water to drink in my name, because ye belong to Christ, verily I say unto you, he shall not lose his reward." (Mark 9:41).

"You were able to earn the money, whereas your brother was not able to earn the money," the daysman will tell Jimmy. He keeps talking to Jimmy until the boy sees how wrong he has been and begins to cry and says to the daysman, "Sir, I'm sorry. I was wrong from the beginning. I am truly sorry. I was ignorant. No one taught me this way. I am very sorry, Mahatmaji, and I'll do anything that you ask me to do. I feel guilty and ashamed from the beginning to the end. What shall I do now to put this thing right?" Jimmy is crying now—his heart is melted—that's a daysman's work.

If you are caught breaking the law and taken into court, the judge will say, "What is wrong, policeman?" The policeman says, "Sir, at such and such a time last night I found this man drunk, breaking a window, and stealing." "Six months in jail," the judge says, and so the case is disposed. But any fool can say, "Six months in jail," or any fool can say, "This man is wrong." Any fool can punish a wrong doer, but it takes a gracious man to love the wrongdoer. Jesus loved us, when he could have thrown all of us into hell. But because He loved us, He died for us! Can't we show as much love towards our next door neighbor? That's the idea that the daysman has.

The daysman now turns to me—he is through with Jimmy, who by now is weeping his heart out. "Look here, Johnny," he'll say to me, "Your brother gave you the money. You could have given him his money back, even if you had only paid him back 10¢ a day. But you had no intention of paying him. You went to him in time of need, and he helped you. You should be grateful to him, but instead, you caused him to get angry. If he had not been angry, he would not have hit you. You did not show gratitude. Suppose Jimmy had died, you would have had to pay every penny to God. "Be not deceived; God is not mocked: for whatsoever a man soweth, that shall he also reap!" The daysman will talk that way to me— he'll show me scripture—he'll convince me of my wrong-doing. He'll make my heart melt, even though it may take several hours to do it. He doesn't have to hurry, because he has all the time in the world.

Now we are both crying, and we ask, "What shall we do?"

"Now Jimmy," he'll say, "Do you feel sorry?"

"Yes sir, very much so."

"Then," the daysman will say, "You fall at Johnny's feet and kiss them." So Jimmy will fall at my feet and kiss them. Kissing the feet is an Eastern expression of not only confessing your guilt, but also the willingness to be reconciled. Let me repeat again—kissing the feet means two things, your confession of guilt, and your willingness to be reconciled to the person that you have wronged. That's why it says in Psalm 2:12, "Kiss the Son, lest he be angry." Then again, you read in the Book, Luke 7:36 to 39, of the woman that came and kissed the feet of Jesus; she didn't ask for forgiveness, but the fact that she kissed His feet meant that she was asking for forgiveness. You read the story in the Book.

So you see that kissing the feet means that you are confessing your sins. You don't have to say anything with your mouth. Kissing the feet also means that you are willing to reconcile yourself with the person you have wronged. So Jimmy kissed my feet, and although he didn't say a word, he is asking my forgiveness. He will keep on kissing my feet until I say, "I've forgiven you." When I give him my forgiveness, he will stop kissing my feet.

Then the daysman will ask me to fall at Jimmy's feet and kiss his feet, because the daysman has shown us that we were both wrong—we have both done evil. That's the philosophy of the daysman. So I fall at Jimmy's feet and kiss his feet until he, too, says, "I forgive you." Then the daysman will bring in some food that has salt in it, and he will have us dip in the same dish and partake and eat of this sacramental food. By this covenant of salt, we pledge to each other that what has gone on in the past will never be remembered. We each begin a new creation, as we eat the salt-containing food together. We are now brothers, as though nothing wrong had ever happened between us. When the disciples asked the Lord, in Matthew 26:22 and 23, "Is it I," who shall betray thee? Jesus answered and said, "He that dippeth his hand with me in the dish, the same shall betray me." Once you dip your hand in the dish and eat together, you can never remember the past. You forget it, it is all buried. You have become new, as though nothing had happened between you.

Then the daysman will say to me, "Johnny, that doesn't mean that you do not owe him the money, you know. You are forgiven, and your guilt is wiped out, but you still owe him the money. When are you going to pay him?"

Then I say, "Well, I will pay him as soon as I get work."

The daysman says, "Well, that may take a long time, and I want to help you out." So the daysman takes money from his own pocket and pays Jimmy the money that I owe him. Then he tells me, "Now forget the debt. I have paid it for you, and you don't owe me a thing. I want you to start off good, so now you don't owe anybody."

So Job said, "For he (God) is not a man, as I am, that I should answer him, and we should come together in judgment." God is in heaven, and I'm down below. God is a spirit, and I am flesh. If God were a man, I could take Him to the elders of the gate, or to the daysman. If the issue were between man and man, I could take him to either of the three places for judgment, but God is not a man. "Neither is there any daysman betwixt us, that might lay his hand upon us both." What Job needed was someone who could lay one hand upon God, and the other hand around Job's shoulders. But Job had no such daysman. We praise God, however, that the daysman did come to this world some time after the dilemma of Job. Job was looking for a daysman when there was no daysman, but he did have faith in a daysman who could reconcile him to God.

The daysman that Job looked for, but did not have, we now have in our Christ. He is the daysman for the whole world, the mediator between God and man. He is the one who paid the debt of the whole world to God, his Father, and he is the one to whom we owe all our gratitude and implicit submission. We love him, because, when no one else was able to reconcile us to God, the Father, Jesus Christ came. Our heavenly daysman, our Lord Jesus Christ, came in due time and redeemed us from death.

Oh, that the world, yea, even all the burdened souls might abandon all their own methods of salvation and turn their eyes to the Redeemer of mankind, the Advocate with the Father, the Daysman, the Daystar, the Altogether Lovely One, and find in him that rest and peace which the world longs for, and which we could not obtain in any other way. The Word of God tells us that, "—there is none other name under heaven given among men, whereby we must be saved." There is only one name, only one God ordained name, in whom, by whom, all that call upon Him might not only be forgiven all their debts, but also might be reconciled to God the Father, against whom they have sinned.

Jesus is still calling us, saying, "Come unto me, and I will give you rest." We don't have to be seeking for a daysman, and we don't have to live in darkness and ignorance. We know that Jesus is here, and that we can be saved by turning ourselves over to Him. It is up to you, beloved reader, to look to this mighty Saviour of the world, the great Daysman, and find in Him, all for which your soul longs.

God bless you, good night.

THE SYCAMORE TREE

Many of you people wonder why I am in America. I am here in America to tell you about the people of the East. The reason I tell you about the people of the East is because the Bible is an Eastern book, in which the incidents are told as the Easterner tells them, and in which the people live in the Eastern way of living. It is my privilege to tell you these things in order that you might become more appreciative and understanding of the Eastern way of thinking and living. My purpose is to enlighten the Western people in regard to the Eastern way of thinking and living, as is recorded in the Bible. I will not speak of anything of the East that does not relate to what is found written in God's Holy Word.

I want to talk on verses 5 and 6 of the 17th chapter of the Gospel of Luke, which says, "And the apostles said unto the Lord, Increase our faith. And the Lord said, If ye had faith as a grain of mustard seed, ye might say unto this sycamine tree, Be thou plucked up by the root, and be thou planted in the sea; and it should obey you." Here you can see how the Eastern people speak and think. The disciples ask the Lord to increase their faith; He answers by bringing in two apparently unrelated things, the mustard seed and the sycamine tree!

The Lord could have answered their request in one of several ways; He could have said that "they had enough faith," or He could have said that "I will give you more faith," or He could have said that "He wouldn't give them any faith," but, because He was a man of the East, talking to men of the East, He answered them in the

35

way that they would understand. He spoke of the mustard seed; now what is mustard seed?

The mustard seed of the East is the smallest of all the seeds, is black, and can be put into an eye, and the person not be aware that the seed is in his eye. But the mustard seed of the East does grow into a tree, as big as the apple trees in America. That's why Jesus said, in Luke 13:19, "It is like a grain of mustard seed, which a man took, and cast into his garden; and it grew, and waxed a great tree; and the fowls of the air lodged in the branches of it."

So your mustard seed is nothing like the mustard seed of the East, neither is your plant anything like the tree-like mustard plant of the East. That's why Kipling said, "East is East, and West is West, and never the twain shall meet." The flowers and fruits, and even the animals are different from yours. To illustrate, I like to go horse back riding, and while I was in England, three or four of my friends asked me to go on my first English horse back ride with them. The horse got to galloping too fast and I wanted to slow it down, so I said to the horse, as we do in India, "Tch, tch." All the Arabian horses of the East are taught to stop when you say "Tch, Tch," and to go when you say, "whoa." So I was saying "tch, tch," and the horse was going faster all the time. One girl in the group, who had been born in India saw my predicament, and ran up near me and yelled, "Don't say like you do in India—say "whoa." So I told the horse "whoa," and it stopped right now! So even our common animals have different mannerisms and are different from yours.

So Jesus said, "If ye had faith as a grain of mustard seed, ye might say unto this sycamine tree, Be thou plucked up by the root, and be thou planted in the sea; and it should obey you." What has the sycamine tree got to do with the mustard seed, and what has the mustard seed to do with faith? Let us first consider the sycamine tree, and see what type of a tree that is in the East. In America, a sycamore tree is a huge tree, that doesn't produce fruit, but in the East, a sycamore tree is about the size and shape of the English pear or English plum tree. The sycamine tree of the East is the wild fig tree, and six times a year it produces fruit. But the people of the East despise this fruit, and won't eat it. Why this is, I don't know, but even if a man has had nothing to eat for two weeks, he wouldn't want to be seen under the sycamine tree, for fear people would think that he was gathering the fruit. And if a man climbed up into a sycamine tree, the people would insult him more. They'd say among themselves, "Poor old Smith must have gone bankrupt overnight. He must not have been eating for weeks and weeks. His poverty is so great that he has lost all self-respect and all his dignity, to be climbing up in a sycamine tree to gather the fruit."

So we read in the 19th chapter of Luke about Zacchaeus climbing up in the sycamore tree to see Jesus when he passed that way, because he was little of stature. But if he wanted to get up above the crowd to see Jesus, why didn't he get up on a house top or get up on a donkey? In the East, if a person wants to see someone pass by, he always gets up on the flat housetops. All our housetops are flat, and anyone can get up on a person's housetop without permission. We never have an inside entrance to get up to the housetops, so that if anyone came and got up on my housetop, I probably would not know about it, and if I did know about it, I would not ask him why he was there. If any important personage is passing by, hundreds of people will get up on the housetops to see him pass. It is much easier to get up on a house top than it would be to get up into one of the sycamore trees of the East.

Many people of the East get up on a camel or a donkey, to get above the crowd and see the people that are passing by. Zacchaeus was a rich man and could easily have offered to get up on a donkey, if he wanted to see Jesus. Also, why didn't he climb some other tree, rather than a sycamore tree, if he wanted to climb a tree to see Jesus? The answer to these points is that Zacchaeus was a rich Pharisee, who, when he heard that Jesus was passing by, thought to himself, "I ought to humble myself. If I get up in the sycamore tree, the people will assume that I am there collecting fruit, and in their heart, they will despise me. They will talk against me, but I don't care, because Jesus will see me there when He passes."

So when Jesus came by, He called to only one man, Zacchaeus. He didn't call to any on the housetops; He didn't call to any on the camels or donkeys; He called to only one man, Zacchaeus! Why?

Jesus called to Zacchaeus because he saw him up in the sycamore tree, and He knew how greatly he had humbled himself, by climbing up in that tree. Jesus once said, "Whosoever therefore shall humble himself as this little child, the same is greatest in the kingdom of heaven." (Matthew 18:4) So Jesus noticed this humble man, and exalted him. I do not know whether you appreciate this act of Zacchaeus, this humility of Zacchaeus, as much as I do or not, but he expressed a tremendous humility. All the people said, "Poor old Zacchaeus, he has hit bottom. He once was a rich man, now look at him!"

Jesus, knew what a sacrifice this man had made; Jesus being an Easterner, also knew the humility manifested here by this man; therefore, He called only one man, Zacchaeus, the man in the sycamore tree, and said, "Zacchaeus, make haste, and come down; for today I must abide at thy house." Jesus knew that here was one man who had emptied himself of all pride, and had made room for Him in his heart, because "the Lord looketh on the heart." (1 Samuel 16:7). Zacchaeus had gotten rid of all his superiority complexes and pride; he knew what the people were saying about him, and he didn't care two hoots. Jesus also knew what the people were saying about this man, so He called, "Make haste and come down."

Again, in the 7th chapter of Amos, mention is made of the sycamore fruit. Amos had been preaching in Israel, and was told to go back to Judah and prophesy there. Then in the 14th verse Amos answered and said, "I was no prophet, neither was I a prophet's son; but I was an herdman, and a gatherer of sycomore fruit." In effect, Amos was saying that he was doing the most menial of all work. But God raised him up into a prophet! God has chosen the foolish things, the weak things, the base things, even a man who gathers sycamore fruit, to bring to naught things that are; that no flesh should glory in his presence! God always chooses the "good for nothing" people, and makes them somebody, and sets them on the house tops, warning man to flee from the wrath to come. In this day, when revival comes, it is going to come through somebody that God has chosen who is gathering sycamore fruit, whose name is not known to society at all, who has never been to school! That somebody, God will call, God will save, God will sanctify, God will fill with the Holy Ghost, and God will send him to the housetops that he may declare the counsel of God, and kings and kingdoms will tremble. That is what is going to happen! Revival is not going to come to any odds and ends of religion, but revival is going to come right from a man of God through the Word, through an Ezekiel, through a John, through an Amos, who was no good! That is God's way, to pick somebody who is no good, and make him somebody!

So then, what did Jesus mean when He said, "If ye had faith as a grain of mustard seed, ye might say unto this sycamine tree, Be thou plucked up by the root, and be thou planted in the sea; and it should obey you." Although the sycamine tree is a small tree, it has enormous, innumerable roots. There are so many roots spread far and wide and deep, that it is impossible to pluck a sycamine tree with all its roots with any of the modern gadgets, without leaving some of the roots behind. But, with faith the size of a mustard seed, it is possible to perform two miracles; first, to pluck the sycamine tree with all its roots; and second, to plunge it into the sea. One act of faith, the size of a mustard seed, will perform two impossible things. This is possible for any of us, if we have the faith.

Many believers will say, "I have not got that much faith." But a believer must never say that, because you have that much faith, otherwise how were you saved? The only way to be saved is to be saved by faith. You were saved by faith, and if you say, "I am saved," then you have faith! When you have faith enough to be saved, which is the first miracle, then you have faith enough to solve all of your problems also. That faith is still in you, because the Christ, that you have received by faith, is still in you. This is the truth that Jesus was telling the disciples, that you don't need an increase of faith, because if you have only a small faith, you can say to the sycamine tree to be plucked up, and it will obey you. With what faith the believer has, he can do the seeming impossible!

Oh, my dear brothers and sisters, so many of us talk about our problems and complain about our problems, but do you have as many problems as the sycamine tree has roots? So many of us think that our problems are too numerous, or too big for the Lord to solve, but let us look at the sycamine roots, thousands of them, some as thick as my thumb, and others as thin as my hair; some are deep, very deep, but by faith you can pluck them all up. So, no matter how deep, how old, how big, how numerous your difficulties are; no matter how big a debt you have; no matter how big a cancer you have; no matter what the doctors have told you about it; no matter how rude your children are; no matter how big or how many enemies you have; no matter how little money you have, you can't have as many problems as a sycamine tree has roots! Our problems are similar to the roots of the sycamine tree, in that if we have a little faith, we can tell our problems, "Be thou plucked up in the name of Jesus," and they will be plucked up and solved in His name!

You are thinking, "It might have happened to the sycamore tree, but my problems are too big." Don't say that. Don't limit yourself, and don't exalt your troubles. By talking about our small troubles, they became bigger and bigger and bigger, and pretty soon we will say, "I don't think that God can save me now." Many of us limit and underestimate the power of Christ, and a believer should never be guilty of that! Believe in an all powerful Christ who can solve your problems, take your problems to Him expecting Him to solve them, and when he does solve them, give God the glory, and give Christ the glory! Remember, no problem has as many roots as a sycamine tree.

God bless you, good night.

THE DOUBLE

"Comfort ye, comfort ye my people, saith your God. Speak ye comfortably to Jerusalem, and cry unto her, that her warfare is accomplished, that her iniquity is pardoned: for she hath received of the Lord's hand double for all her sins." (Isaiah 40:1, 2). This means that she has received of the Lord's hand double—not twice as much, but double. Not double in our sense of the word, but a clean account; a paid-up account, where nothing can be held against her whatsoever!

Picture in your mind, if you please, a piece of paper, on one side of which is written all the names of a man's creditors and the amounts owed. Fold that paper in two, double it with the clean white sides of the paper on the outside, and give it to the debtor. Then this debtor will have received of the creditors double—a clean sheet—a fully paid-up account.

When we come to the Lord Jesus Christ and receive the "double" from His hand, all is blotted out. "There is therefore now no condemnation to them which are in Christ Jesus." (Romans 8:1). "Blotting out the handwriting of ordinances that was against us, which was contrary to us, and took it out of the way, nailing it to his cross." (Colossians 2:14). Everything that was against us is blotted out by the blood of the Lord Jesus Christ— "Blotting out the handwriting that was against us."

When we come to Jesus Christ, we get a complete pardon; we become a new creation. Old things are passed away—thrown behind His back—never to be remembered. We get a clean sheet; we begin a new life just as though we never committed any sin against anybody at any time! Our sins are blotted out; that is what Jesus Christ does. WONDERFUL SAVIOUR ! ! ! Jesus never remembers anything against us, because there is nothing to remember. He paid it all! He paid the debt! That which we couldn't pay, He paid; and the price He paid was His own precious blood!

Therefore, we have a clean sheet from Him. Any down and out person, any discouraged person, ANY person, can look to Jesus Christ and say, "I put up my hand and receive double from your good hands. I can't redeem myself and I can't pay my debt; I cannot fulfill my obligation. Oh, Lord, I strived and I labored, and the more I tried, the deeper I sank." The Lord Jesus Christ will give him the double, will save his soul and set him free. He becomes a new creation from then on!

So we, who have received the double for our portion, have a clean life, a dynamic life, a life of fruit bearing. One of these fruits is love, but other people don't see anything different in us! Nobody has ever criticized Christ yet. They will criticize Christianity, they will criticize pastors, but not Christ. I have never heard one person in the East or West criticizing Christ's life. The moment anyone mentions Christ, the whole world is drawn to Him in their hearts. But the moment that you mention Christian people, then quarrels begin. Once the name of Christ is mentioned, then love starts operating. I travel a lot, and I know how much the Hindus appreciate and admire Christ—not Christians—but Christ. We, who have received the double in our lives, must begin to demonstrate the love of God to other people through our lives. We should manifest the love of Christ to us by our love to other people and their problems!

THE EAGLES

Now turn to Isaiah 40:29, 30, and 31. "He giveth power to the faint; and to them that have no might he increaseth strength. Even the youths shall faint and be weary, and the young men shall utterly fall: but they that wait upon the Lord shall renew their strength; they shall mount up with wings as eagles; they shall run, and not be weary; and they shall walk, and not faint."

Psalm 103:5 reads, "Who satisfieth thy mouth with good things; so that thy youth is renewed like the eagle's."

And again, Micah 1:16 says, "Make thee bald, and poll thee for thy delicate children; enlarge thy baldness as the eagle. . ."

Keep these three references in mind and let us consider them. "They that wait upon the Lord shall renew their strength; they shall mount up with wings as eagles." There are two kinds of eagles in the East, one is a "holy" eagle, and the other is a "dirty" eagle. The dirty eagles are those that gather around any dead carcass; they gather to eat of it, and are the wild vultures. We, in the East, call them "dirty" eagles. Jesus said, in Matthew 24:28, "For wheresoever the carcase is, there will the eagles be gathered together." In this passage, Jesus referred to the dirty eagles or vultures, because where the dead body is, there are the vultures eating and picking it. When a fasting Hindu breaks his fast, the first thing that he wants to look at is a holy eagle. If this Hindu who is looking for a holy eagle sees a dirty eagle instead, he goes back and fasts again. To the Hindu, it is an evil omen to break a fast without seeing a HOLY eagle.

The dirty eagles are always roaming around in the gutters somewhere. The dirty eagles are equal to carnal Christians; they are always looking to things, things, things, things, things. Their vision is not high enough, neither can they see high enough, because their faith is not high enough. They are always down on the floor, looking for things and for pleasures. That is why the vultures are like carnal Christians—I don't like to call them Christians, but they are carnal. They are looking for the husks that the swine did eat, having pleasure in things, things, things. They very seldom look to the Spirit, but look to things all the time.

They are like vultures, dirty, filthy, unsatisfying; they are miserable to themselves, a misery to others, nauseating to themselves and to others! Why? Because they are looking to THINGS all the time and not to the Spirit. THINGS never satisfy—the SPIRIT always does! We who are Christians must not walk according to the flesh, but we must walk according to the Spirit. There are many saved Christians who have walked according to the flesh from the time that they got saved; they were saved by the Spirit, but they walk by the flesh. But we who have taken Jesus Christ as our Lord and Saviour are not supposed to walk according to the flesh; we are supposed to walk according to the Spirit! This is the reason Christians are so unhappy, and this is the reason that their husbands, and wives, and fathers and mothers aren't impressed with them.

Now the holy eagles, what are they? The holy eagles never eat anything that is dead; they always pick up live things for food. They build their nests in the tops of the coconut palms, maybe 80 or 90 feet off of the ground.

The holy eagles are like unto the church of God—the real believers who are saved by faith and walk by faith; the believers whose home is not in this world, but whose home is heavenward. A real believer sets his affections on things above, not on things below! A real believer is seated in heavenly places NOW! That's right, NOW! If you would only realize this fact, you would not have one moment of misery. We are only earth-bound in body—in spirit we are seated with Him on the throne. The Bible says, "Even when we were dead in sins, (God) hath quickened us together with Christ, (by grace are ye saved); and hath raised us up together, and made us sit together in heavenly places in Christ Jesus." (Ephesians 2:5, 6). Fancy a man like you or me, seated on a throne up there and listening to heavenly things—that is a glorious position, you know! The bulk of the Christians are not taught all these things, because it is too supernatural for them. Yet for the real believers, these facts are natural! We are seated in heavenly places with Christ Jesus; we were crucified with Him; we were buried with Him; we arose with Him; we ascended with Him when He ascended; and we are now seated with Him in heavenly places. This is very wonderful and very thrilling if you believe it. Believing brings results, but just thinking brings no results—let us begin believing right now! Praise the Lord!

The holy eagles are likened to heavenly beings; they are the "king of birds." Once every five, ten or fifteen years, (people differ on the time interval) the eagles build a nest high in the coconut tree, and then abandon themselves, like advanced swimmers that dive into the water. So these eagles, right from the coconut palm, abandon themselves and dive down into a lake, or pond or well, or any still water. They dive headfirst, with their wings folded intact on their back—they don't fly down. They abandon themselves with their heads down and we see them all dropping into the water. Soon after going into the water, they come to the top, having lost every single feather. When they go in, they have all their feathers;

when they come to the top, the feathers are floating on the water, and these poor birds have lost every feather. They are helplessly stranded in the water, because without feathers they can't fly, and they never could swim. What happens now to these poor eagles?

They struggle and do the best that they can to reach the shore. When they get to the rocks and sand, the people come and feed the eagles with food, because the Eastern people look upon them as holy eagles, representative of God. They feed them with rice and other food, and the eagles stay there helplessly. Nobody will hurt them because they look upon them as heavenly beings. Then in six or seven weeks' time, their new feathers have grown out, and they fly back. Nothing can stop them now. That is why "they that wait upon the Lord SHALL renew their strength; they SHALL mount up with wings as eagles."

The eagles lose their feathers first, then they wait! While waiting, they live on what they can get—they get their new feathers and THEN they fly. "They that wait upon the Lord shall renew their strength; they shall mount up with wings as eagles; they shall run, and not be weary; and they shall walk, and not faint." So where is your old age? People are always talking about being old, and saying, "I am old." If you want to become young, you must lose all your old feathers—your old feathers of negativism, and your old feathers of limitations! "I can't do it," is a very bad expression, you know. "I can't do it," and "I can't see it," are all negative feathers. The Christian's thought is, "I CAN do all things through Christ who strengthens me!" This is a positive feather. We are born with a spoon of "can't" in our mouth. "I can't, I can't, I can't." When you come to Jesus Christ you say, "I can give anything." When you say, "I can," you will be on the mountain tops all the time. Then everyone in your town will get saved, as they see that you are really doing something for Jesus!

When we come to the Lord Jesus Christ, we must examine ourselves, because before we come, we must be willing to say, "Lord, break me, melt me, mold me and take away any wicked feather of unbelief in my heart and in my personality, and remove any old feathers that have made me weak and brought me into limitations." A Christian has NO limitations, because Christ has none! A Christian can do anything he wants to do, but generally, the Christian doesn't WANT to do anything! That's the big reason why a Christian doesn't DO anything!

A Christian loses all his feathers when he comes to Christ, because "old things are passed away; behold all things are become new." (II Corinthians 5:17). "I am crucified with Christ: nevertheless I live; yet not I, but Christ liveth in me," Paul says, "and the life which I now live in the flesh I live by. . . . ?" Did Paul say, "By sight"? Did he say, "by religion"? NO SIR! He said, "I live by the faith of the Son of God, who loved me, and gave himself for me." (Galatians 2:20). Is it any wonder that we can't make both ends meet, when we try to live by sight, and by things? We, who have been saved, are to live by faith, and not by sight; by the Spirit, and not by flesh. When we live by the Spirit, we can say, "I can do all things through Christ which strengtheneth me." (Philippians 4:13). When you come to the Lord Jesus Christ, the Lord convicts you of how many old feathers you have.

Each person knows his own hindering feathers; maybe it is anger, maybe malice, maybe selfishness, maybe criticism, maybe gossip, maybe self-centeredness; or it may be some other dirty old feather hanging onto you!

When we come to Him, the Holy Ghost will put His finger on the feather, and we must be willing to throw it off. After we have thrown away all the old feathers that have been holding us from blessings, THEN WE WAIT ON GOD! We can't wait on God and ask for new feathers, when we still have all our old dirty ones!

We must, therefore, empty ourselves before He can fill us. In II Kings, chapter 4, when the widow was in debt, Elijah told her to bring all the empty vessels and start pouring oil into them. She had only one pot of oil in the house when she began to pour. But as many vessels as her son brought, the Lord was able to fill, and yet there was oil to fill more. As the woman was pouring, the oil was increasing in the pot. Today as you pour and pour more oil, God gives the increase.

Hallelujah! That is what God does with our income, with our business. If we are clogged up with our self-importance, the other self-made feathers which have given us a headache and a heartache all our lives, and we don't want to get rid of them, how can God bless us? He can only give us new feathers in place of the old ones, if we lose the old ones. He can fill an empty pot, but He can't fill a full pot—it is already full.

That is why the eagles have better sense than we do. The eagles don't pray, "Lord, these four feathers are getting old. I want to lose only these feathers, Lord, because the others still look good to me. So please let me lose four old ones and you give me four new ones." But that is what we Christians do, isn't it?

Some people say, "Well, I drink cocktails. Occasionally I take a glass of wine and see no harm in that—I'd like to hang onto that feather. There is no harm in it. But, Lord, while I want to keep the cocktails, give me some Holy Ghost at the same time." How foolish!

The eagle might have said, "God can do a half-and-half job; suppose I lose four old ones and you give me four new ones, maybe next week I can lose two more feathers because they are getting old, too." But instead, the eagle says, "Why don't I make a clean breast of the whole thing and become a new creation?" So you should say, "I am going to abandon my feathers." Then down you go to the water, and God helps you, and the feathers come out somehow. Then you wait in humility and meekness at the mercy of the people. As you wait, God does His work giving all new feathers, not just four or five feathers, but ALL ! ! ! He can do this because ALL of the old ones are lost.

If you lose only four feathers, you will fly a little better, but not as well as you should, because the other old ones are still hanging on. That is why Christian people are sometimes gloomy and most of them are depressed. They can't walk; they can't fly; they can't talk. They get tired with every little step. Why don't they want new strength to come to them?

Because they don't want to lose the old rags and the old feathers.

That's why I don't believe in old age. Our people in India live to be 165 and 175 years old. These so-called "pagans" live to 165 years of age. And we, who are Christians, as soon as we are forty-five, become nervous wrecks, and complain about, "My poor old nerves." When we are forty-seven, we lose our hair, and when we are forty-eight our backs give out, and we go to bed and live like parasites and say, "Praise the Lord, the Lord put me here. This is my cross to bear."

What a lie that is! The Lord never gave you such a cross. Our only cross in this world, my friends, is not suffering, although many great saints are suffering, but our cross is to bear witness to Jesus Christ—a cross of joy and peace. It is not the fault of God that we suffer, because when Christ was wounded, He was wounded for all our sicknesses. All our sicknesses were laid upon

Him, therefore don't say, "It is my cross." Don't bring in about Paul's thorn in the flesh, because poor old Paul never had any sickness, people just think he had, that's all. You see, the children of Israel, when they walked for forty years in the wilderness, had no doctors, only God. There was not one feeble one among them, the Book says. There was no sickness. They died for their unbelief, that's true; because they asked for death, they got it. They got what they wanted, and we are getting what we want. "As a man thinketh in his heart, so is he." You can't change that law, so be careful what you think! Think only what you want to happen. Oh, my dear brothers and sisters, I am so glad that we are getting these points today.

We should either quit calling ourselves Christians or else start practicing our faith, because we can't carry on this wretched old religion bringing disgrace upon the church of God. Let us try to think RIGHT! What do you want to be? Do you want to have a happy, prosperous, contented life? Then think so, and such will be your lot, God being your helper, your Saviour, and your Lord.

Now, "They that wait upon the Lord shall renew their strength; they shall mount up with wings as eagles." We wait upon the Lord, getting rid of all our negative feathers, all of the feathers of limitations which we imposed upon ourselves. You can become a new creation this minute, and can get rid of the old feathers NOW! The moment that you say, "Yes, Lord, I do," that moment the old feathers are gone, and then He will give you all new ones. What are the new ones He gives you? He gives love, joy, peace, long-suffering, gentleness, goodness, faith, meekness and temperance. He gives you all these. From that time on, you can live like a monarch, like a prince, an heir and joint-heir with Christ. Every place you look is yours, whatever you look at is yours, anything you see is yours.

I can give you many examples: I know a man who has a daughter and he and the daughter often go shopping. I have gone with them many times, and this is the story of the shopping tour: The daughter will be picking up some things in the shop while the father is buying something in another part of the store. When she has picked up the things she wants, she waits for her father to look her way, then she simply shows the father what she has picked out. Does she plead with him, "Father, can I buy this?" Of course not! She simply smiles at her father, holding the stuff she has bought. She doesn't need to ask him; she just smiles and gets all of the stuff. The daughter just smiles at the father and the father pays the bill.

Don't you do the same with your children when you take them shopping? How you love your children! When the child wants anything, you say, "Yes, sonny you may get that. All right, here it is, buy it." "If ye then, being evil, know how to give good gifts unto your children: HOW MUCH MORE shall your heavenly Father give the Holy Spirit to them that ask him?" (Luke 11:13). It is always thus with Jesus. "HOW MUCH MORE, HOW MUCH MORE, HOW MUCH MORE?" "They that wait upon the Lord shall renew their strength; they shall mount up with wings as eagles; they shall run, and not be weary; and they shall walk, and not faint." (Isaiah 40:31).

Men ninety years old in India, can walk and carry a heavy bag. Ninety year old men in India do not lose their teeth even at that age. What's happening to us in America? Even before we are sixteen we start going to the dentist. What's wrong with us? We don't live right, that's all! We are Christians; we are saved, oh, yes! We are saved all right; we are not going to hell—we are going to heaven, but we live in hell here. We are going to heaven all right—sometime later, but we can't find heaven here. Why? We have too many old feathers and we don't like to lose them. "They that wait upon the Lord shall renew their strength."—Hallelujah. "They shall mount up with wings as eagles." Wings will come only when you wait, and you can wait only if you have dropped the old feathers.

At one time in India there was a man and his wife who were saved; and their son, who was possibly five or six years old, fell ill. Some of my pastors went and prayed for him. (We believe in anointing with oil in our church). My pastor told me, "Bishop, we have been praying for a boy who is ill. He doesn't eat anything; we don't know what the trouble is. They are Christians and all the village folks think that is why their son fell ill. Other people who want to be saved are hesitating now; they think if they come to Christ, their children will fall ill, too."

That same kind of thing goes on here in America. If a believer loses some business after he is saved, everybody talks about it. "Oh, he is a Christian—that's why it happened that way!" In that case we should not get upset. That is only a stepping-stone to greater faith. "All things work together for good to them that love God." That is the truth that we should know when things go wrong.

So I went to pray for this boy at his home; he lived in a small mud hut. He was sitting up. There were several pastors with me, and the father and mother of the boy were there. As I was talking, I was praying, "Lord, what is wrong? You said that if we should ask anything in your name, you would do it. These pastors have been praying. This whole community, Lord, is ripe for salvation. For your own glory, Lord, please let me know what is hindering; which feather it is that is hindering this boy from being healed." While everybody was talking to

me, I was talking like that to the Lord. You can talk that
way to God; it is easy to do!

All of a sudden, as soon as they had finished talking
to me, I got the answer from the Lord. The boy, by this
time, was lying down, and I noticed that they had on his
arm one of those pillows that I have talked to you about
—some native witch doctor had brought it in to the
parents. The Christian parents were asking the pastors
to pray, and at the same time, they were hanging on to
the old feather of the witch doctors. That was what was
hindering. The pastors did not have the wisdom to see
it, but God revealed it to me. I said to the parents, "The
pastors have been praying for your boy. Have you also
been going to the witch doctors, to your old religious
doctors, for anything?

They said, trembling, "Yes, sir."

"That is the thing that is hindering," I said. "God will
have all the glory to himself. He will not share it with
the devil, or with anyone." So I told the father of the
boy, "If you will remove this pillow, your boy will be
healed now." He removed it, and I told him to burn it,
so that it wouldn't be put back, and he did.

"Will you promise me that you won't go back to the
devil for your boy, for anything? Will you promise that
you will trust only in the Lord?"

"Yes," the mother and father both said.

I put my hand on the boy's head and prayed, "Lord,
thank you for revealing the exact feather to which they
were hanging. So Lord, please heal this boy. Thank you,
Lord, for the healing, Amen."

I believe in healing. Every Christian ought to believe
in healing. You can't believe one part of the Bible and
just forget the rest of the Bible. We have to believe all
or none! As soon as I got back home the boy began to

eat a meal. A servant came from the boy's house saying, "Why was he healed now, and not before?" When the feather of unbelief was shaken off, a new feather came!

Why hang on to the feather of unbelief, anyway?

Why hang on to the feather of selfishness, anyway?

Why hang on to the feather of doubt, anyway?

Why hang on to the feather of self-centeredness, anyway? They are all dirty feathers; you will sink with them hanging on to you. Why sink? YOU ARE SAVED TO LIVE! Christians are always talking about dying, you know. They sing in that hymn, "When we all get to heaven, what a day of rejoicing that will be." But what about rejoicing now! We sing some awful hymns, don't we? We sing that when we get to heaven we'll all have a crown, but we don't have a dollar bill in our pockets now! Why have a crown of gold on your head there, and not have some gold in your pocket here? God gives us gold now, and afterwards, a crown!

You see, when Jesus comes into our heart and life, we become new creatures but we can also go back and pick up, one by one, the old rags and the old feathers again after we are saved, and stick them back on again if we wish. We can be unwilling to throw them away. One man came up to see me at the railroad station and said, "Bishop, I want to talk to you, but not here in front of everybody." So we went out, and he said, "Bishop, I have been saved for a long time, fourteen or fifteen years, and all this time I have been hanging onto cigarette smoking."

This man was burdened about this, and went on, "I have made promises to stop smoking many times. I have burned up my cigarettes. I have made promises to my wife and to my children, but these promises only lasted ten or fifteen minutes, and then the devil would come to me and tell me to take a cigarette. I have been very burdened, Bishop, and I would give anything if I could get the victory. I smoke a terrible amount, and I know it is a waste of money—God's money, and my children's money."

"Shall I tell you the truth about it?" I asked. "Will you be offended? The trouble with you is that you are not willing to give up on the inside. Deep down in your heart, you are not willing to stop smoking. You wish that God would overlook it. You are taking a shelter in your weakness; you are not taking a shelter in your stronghold, Jesus Christ! You are taking shelter in yourself, and so you are sinking! You must lift the center from yourself, and put it in Jesus, then the power comes! In other words, you must get rid of the old dirty feathers of praying selfishly."

This Christian man said that his consecration lasted only ten or fifteen minutes, and that he prayed and prayed. Nonsense! He didn't pray; he only prayed to keep it going, that's all. Look, the eagles don't pray from the coconut palm, "Lord, I am poor and weak; there is no harm in having old feathers, Lord. After all's said and done, you created my feathers. They're weak, but that's my cross, Lord. Just let me suffer in it." They don't pray that way!

That language is the language of human beings. Eagles show better sense and better language. That is why they are called heavenly eagles. They know that the only way to get rid of the old feathers is to abandon themselves. You abandon yourself to the Lord Jesus Christ and God will give YOU all new feathers, my dearly beloved friend.

Good night, and God bless you!

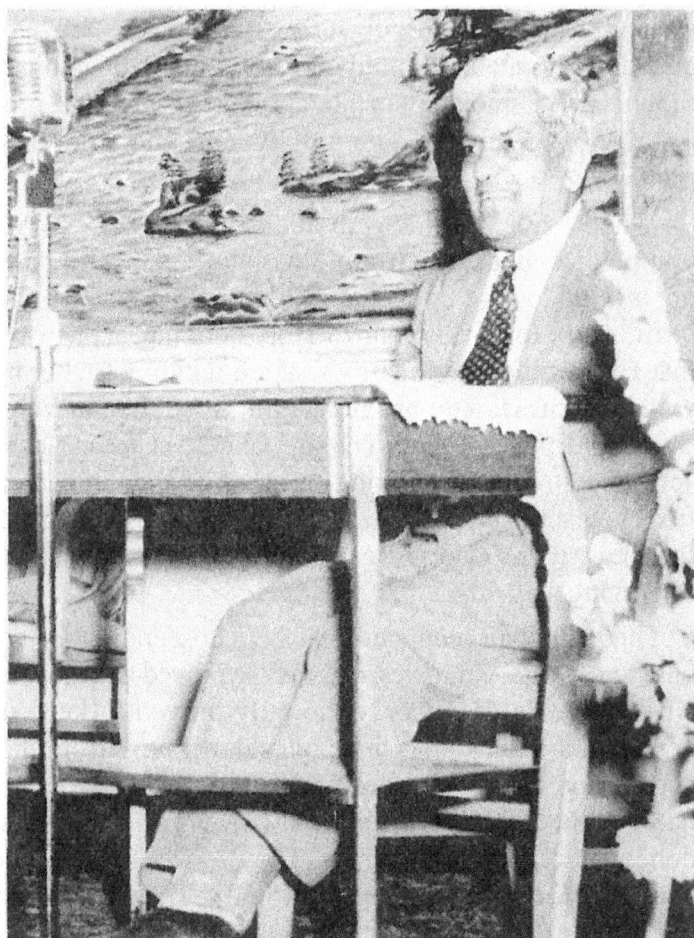

BLIND BARTIMAEUS

Let us turn to the Gospel according to St. Mark, chapter 10, beginning at verse 46 and read to the end of the chapter, "And they came to Jericho: and as he went out of Jericho with his disciples and a great number of people, blind Bartimaeus, the son of Timaeus, sat by the highway side begging. And when he heard that it was Jesus of Nazareth, he began to cry out, and say: Jesus, thou son of David, have mercy on me. And many charged him that he should hold his peace: but he cried the more a great deal, Thou son of David, have mercy on me. And Jesus stood still, and commanded him to be called. And they call the blind man, saying unto him, Be of good comfort, rise; he calleth thee. And he, casting away his garment, rose, and came to Jesus. And Jesus answered and said unto him, What wilt thou that I should do unto thee? The blind man said unto him, Lord, that I might receive my sight. And Jesus said unto him, Go thy way; thy faith hath made thee whole. And immediately he received his sight, and followed Jesus in the way."

As soon as he had received his sight, he didn't go back to sleep, but he followed Jesus in the way! Many of us have received sight, perhaps, even physical sight, and we forget all about it; but this man followed Jesus "in the way." His way is the only true way—that's why he "followed Jesus in the way." I like these words very much and I'd like to make a comment on it for my own benefit and edification. Many of us who were saved maybe 20 or 30 years ago, did not walk in the way with Jesus. We walked in our own way, but on Sunday morning or Sunday evening when there was a special meeting, then we would try to "walk in the way." Any other way, which is not "THE WAY," is the way of man. The reason that we have all kinds of misery and fear is because, at the time we were saved, we just didn't walk in the way, as it is laid down by His word, in His book. That is the reason why we get into all kinds of entanglements in this world. So tonight, as a result of this meeting, I hope that all of us will walk "in the way." If we receive any special light as a result of this meeting tonight, we should determine to walk in "the way."

Now to go back to verse 50, "And he, casting away his ROBE, rose and came to Jesus." You may ask, "Why don't you accept the word garment"? The reason is because the word "garment" may mean any part of my clothing; it may mean a shirt, or an undergarment, or a tie. It may mean a coat or a vest. Thus the word "garment" means anything. But a "robe" means a distinct garment—a cloak.

Why do I say things that seemingly look contradictory to things that are in the Bible? Some of you may have noticed that I try to take away that which is in the Bible and put in something else. I have explained that enough, but I will say this, that the writers of the Bible were all Western people, who did not understand Eastern culture, and they gave a literal translation from the Aramaic language to the Greek, or from the Hebrew to the Greek, and from the Greek to English. Therefore, when people translate who do not understand the culture of the land, then each word has so many different meanings. To prove this point, there is a passage in the Bible that has just come to my mind that I will bring you. John the Baptist said to the Pharisees that came to be baptized in the river Jordan, "O generation of vipers, who hath warned you to flee from the wrath to come?" (Luke 3:7). This passage should read, "O generation of scorpions," not vipers. There is no sense to it when they say "vipers."

I get my information from the everyday usage of the language of the people in which I was born and raised, and not from the commentaries, which contain a lot of uncertainties, because the authors of the commentaries only guess at what they say. Therefore, you are safe to get information from me, because I won't mislead you, and this information that you get from me will make the Bible more real and more wonderful. So this should be, "O generation of scorpions," instead of "generation of vipers." That's the language we use. That's what John the Baptist used. That's what my grandfather used, and that's the language that I use when I am in the East.

There are two kinds of scorpions, you know. The black scorpions, which are few, precious few, and the blue scorpions, which are plentiful. John the Baptist meant the black scorpions, because in order to use the saying, "O generation of vipers," you always mean the black scorpion. Now the black scorpion has a very peculiar tendency—when the scorpion is conceived, the father dies; when the scorpion is born, the mother dies. The mother dies because the scorpion, from the inside, eats its way out of the mother. By the time the scorpion has eaten its way out, and becomes a little scorpion, the mother dies. Thus there are very few black scorpions, because the father dies when the young one is conceived, and the mother dies when it is born. Thus, in the East, if anybody is unspiritual, unreligious, stomach-minded, materialistic minded, and never thinks of God, we call them a generation of scorpions. Why? Because a scorpion is born an orphan. The scorpion has no one to guide it, or teach it. So a man who is not spiritual is like a scorpion—he has no light, no wisdom, no truth, no teachings and no spirituality. As the black scorpion is born an orphan, so is the man who is born in this world and is not taught the things of the Spirit. We call these men a "generation of scorpions." Such men are only stomach minded; they eat, eat, eat, go to sleep and die. They have no spirituality at all—nobody guides them—they are spiritual orphans.

In Acts, 28:3, the Bible tells about Paul taking up a viper—this is a real viper, and does not mean a scorpion. So you see, in order to translate correctly, you must know the context, and the circumstances of the language and the conditions under which it is used. This is true because in the Aramaic language ONE WORD means FOUR different things. So if you are an Easterner, you know which one of those four words were meant when certain phraseology was used according to certain conditions. If you are a Westerner, translating the Aramaic word, you may not know which one of the four words to choose, so you just pick the word that seems the best to you. This is what has been done in the revised Bible. They revise it, but they don't give you the information you want. Look up this passage in your new revised Bible and see if they tell you the information on this passage of scripture! Why don't they tell you? Because they don't know it, and they don't want to know it! Their attitude is summed up thus, "Keep the poor people blind, because they don't understand it, anyway." The time has come for us to be enlightened, quickened, awakened—to know the real truth. "And ye shall know the truth, and the truth shall make you free," Jesus said. (John 8:32).

Let us go back to the 50th verse again, "And he, casting away his garment, rose, and came to Jesus." He casting away his ROBE, rose, and came to Jesus. I shall explain to you why it is a robe and not a garment, and prove this to you in accordance with the Word of God.

So blind Bartimaeus sat by the highway side begging. But this day, Jesus was passing by, and while he could not see Jesus passing by, he could hear Him. Everywhere Jesus went, there were hundreds of people with him shouting "Hosanna," and "Jesus," and singing.

In the Eastern countries, a great personality, a big man, does not go alone. Wherever Mahatma Gandhi went, there were thousands upon thousands of people lined up for hundreds of miles just to look at him passing by. Many people walked barefoot for two whole days, just to see Mahatma Gandhi passing by in the train. So, in the time of Jesus Christ, whenever he went by, there were so many people with Him that the whole countryside could hear Him passing that way.

When Jesus got close, this blind man, who was named Bartimaeus, began calling out, "Jesus, thou son of David, have mercy on me." Many around him told him, "Hey, keep quiet," but he would not keep quiet, because he believed this was all the opportunity that he had. Jesus was passing by and He was the only one who could give him his sight! Bartimaeus would not be stopped. He cried the more, a great deal.

When you ask something of God, don't keep on asking the same old thing, but thank God, as though you had received it, and you will get it. Jesus said, "What things soever ye desire, when ye pray, believe that ye receive them, and ye shall have them." (Mark 11:24). Either Jesus is speaking the truth or He is not speaking the truth when He said this, and I believe, and I know from experience, that He DOES speak the truth. When you don't get an answer to your prayer, don't make God out a liar, but wait patiently, keeping on thanking God for what you are going to get. Then all of a sudden, it will drop in, much more than you expected!

So blind Bartimaeus believed that Jesus alone could

give him his sight, and that this was his only opportunity. He wasn't going to be stopped by anyone. He
cried all the more, a great deal, saying, "Jesus, thou son
of David, have mercy on me." Jesus stood still, of course!
"Him that cometh to me I will in no wise cast out." He
has said, in John 6:37. So, just like Jesus, He stopped
there, when He heard blind Bartimaeus call Him. Jesus
didn't go by the majority opinion; neither did He call a
committee meeting, and say, "Now look here, boys,
should I do anything for this poor blind man? All in
favor of me helping this man, hands up; all opposed,
hands down."

Just because everybody does it, or just because everybody thinks so, doesn't mean that it is right. We often
go by the majority, but we shouldn't do that; we should
go according to the Word of God! In America, everything is run by the majority; and we have a committee
for this and a committee for that. We have committees,
committees, committees, but only a little of Christ. We
must have more of Christ, and less committees. We must
have more prayer, and less organization.

So when Jesus heard blind Bartimaeus call, he stood
still and commanded him to be called. When Jesus said
to go and call him, blind Bartimaeus could not see to
come, of course, but some of the folks came to him and
said, "Be of good comfort, rise; He calleth thee." Then
"he, casting away his robe, rose, and came to Jesus."
Jesus didn't tell him to cast away his robe before he
came; neither did the disciples say to him, "You be a
good fellow, and cast away your robe, and come," but
he did it himself! Why did he do it? What is the sig-
nificance of the casting away of the robe? We'll discuss
all that.

Before we discuss this, though, let me take you to the
East and let me give you the true picture of this man,

Bartimaeus. Of course, I have never seen this man, but the land which is spoken of there tells me all about him. The Scripture says that he sat "by the highway side begging," and also, that he cast away his robe. These two things may not mean much to you, but according to the customs of the East, they tell me more about Bartimaeus than you think.

When you go to the East, you find a lot more beggars there, seemingly, than you do in the West. I want you to remember this point. When you go to Palestine, Egypt or India, you find so many beggars in certain places. Many people in America think that all these beggars are poor people, that's the reason that they are begging, BUT THIS IS NOT SO! The majority of the beggars that sit in certain places and ask for alms are not there for money. They are there, in the attitude of begging, because they seek healing from an incurable condition. In the Eastern philosophy, either Hindu, Mohammedan or Jewish, if a man is incurable, and the doctors have given him up, then he becomes a beggar, seeking not money, but healing.

Suppose that I have a son that is blind. He wasn't born blind, but he has become blind, and I have taken him to the best doctors in India. The doctors finally say to me, "We have done the best we can for your son. There is nothing more that we can do. Only God can heal your son." If you are pronounced a leper and incurable, or if your wife has an incurable condition, then your only recourse is to turn to God for healing. Then, according to religion, in order to get sympathy and favor from God, you must become a beggar. You must act as a beggar.

When you act as a beggar, then you have no more self-respect. You lose all your self-respect, you lose all your social standing, you become the humblest of the humble, when you act as a beggar. Then God, through

His mercy, may give you healing, someway, sometime, through some holy man. That is the kind of a teaching we have in the East.

Thus, in the morning, I dress my blind son up according to the class to which he belongs, and put him in my automobile. If he is a Hindu, I put a turban on his head, and put on clothes, proper to his position, so that even though he cannot see, yet the people passing by will give him due respect, and not insult him. Then I put a wooden bowl in his hand and take him in the automobile to one of three places. The three places where the beggars go are the highway side, where blind Bartimaeus was; the temple gate, or the banks of the holy rivers. Thousands of people go past these three places daily, and we pray that in one of these three places there might be a holy man passing my son, and as he passes, his shade might fall on my boy, or he might say a word that would heal him, or he might touch him and heal him. So, hoping and trusting that God in His mercy might heal my son through his holy man, and with this hope and faith and confidence, I take my son in the morning and put him on the highway side.

Why highway side? The highway side is a place where a lot of caravans go. Thousands of people travel here day and night. If you sat by the side of a small road, you would not see many people passing by, but by a main highway thousands of people pass daily. That's why blind Bartimaeus sat by the highway side. So I put my son by the highway side in the morning, and he will say, "Alms, alms, alms," all day long. The people of the East will look at my son's turban and say, "Oh, he's a cultured man; he's a Hindu; he's the well educated son of a rich father. He's not a pauper, he's not begging alms for bread—don't you see the turban? Oh, dear, dear, the poor boy! All day long he is in the attitude of begging to show his humility." People who understand the culture and the religions of the East will understand that this boy is not there for money, to fill up his stomach with what few coppers that he might get. We of the East understand this! There are hundreds of people lining both sides of the road, in the cities and highway side, wherever you look—the lame, the blind, the lepers, the diseased and the incurables.

But there are a lot of people like you, who go to the East from the Western hemisphere, who do not understand anything about our culture or our religions, and what you do understand is generally all wrong. So you look at all these incurables, at all these cripples, and the first thing that you do is to point your camera at them and take some photographs to send to the folks back home. This American hobby of taking pictures of everything ugly and mean and squalid and sending the pictures back home, is resented in the East. Why don't you take pictures of the nice things; the good looking people, the fine buildings, the beautiful cities? Thus the Western world gets a poor impression of the East, and the East gets a poor impression of the West, because the people of the East see only the Westerner with a camera, taking pictures of the bad things of the East.

So the people from the Western hemisphere come along and see my son begging, and think that he is really begging for money, so they put some pennies in his bowl. But the Westerner doesn't understand the mind of the East, do you see? If he understood the mind of the East, he would know that this boy was not begging for money, but for healing. My purpose for being here in America is to enlighten you and educate you concerning the Eastern people, so that you might understand them, and in understanding them, you might understand the Bible better. I am a spiritual and cultural exchange lecturer, and am here representing no denomination, but only to bring you the Bible and the truth.

So, in the evening, I go out to the highway side, and get my son, and put him in the car, and if there are a few pennies dropped into his bowl, I take that money, before I take my son home, and give it to the really poor. We have plenty of really poor people in the East, of course, and you have plenty of poor people in the Western countries, too. In America, your poor people must not beg openly, but they sit in the street holding pencils, which they never sell. They are really begging, but they are pretending to sell something. People don't buy shoelaces from a blind man; they drop some money in the hat and go on. They never buy the laces; it is the Western way of begging, that's all.

In the East, everything that is done is done according to religion. Our social life is based on religion, and our religion is based on our social life. In the West, social life is one thing, religious life is another, but in the East the social and religious life are inseparable—that's why we can't think unless it's according to our religion. I hope you understand that very important point. The Eastern religion means life, and life means religion. You must understand this point to understand the East! We, in the East, are steeped in religion, our thoughts are based on religion; you in the West have your thoughts on your living standards. That's the big difference between the East and the West, but I like both the East and the West.

The fact that blind Bartimaeus was sitting on the highway side begging, shows me, therefore, that he was not begging for money. The real beggars of the East that beg for food, come to the door. They don't knock on the door, they tap on the floor by the door. Then we know they are beggars, and the woman of the house comes out and gives them something to eat. But the beggars who line the highway side, and who sit at the temple gates, are generally beggars who are seeking healing. What are the temple gates? The temple gates are both sides of the passage to the temple, maybe a hundred sitting on this side of the passage, and a hundred lining the other side. Then all who go to the temple must pass them, both going into and coming out of the temple. So these incurable beggars sit in the temple gates waiting for healing!

Take the case of Peter and John going to the temple, as told in the third chapter of Acts. There they saw a lame man and he asked them for alms. And Peter said, "Silver and gold have I none; but such as I have give I thee: In the name of Jesus Christ of Nazareth rise up and walk." Peter and John, knowing the Eastern mind and the so called "beggars" of the East, understood this case.

They could have given him a penny, but they didn't do it, because they knew why he was there. They used a good old Eastern way of speaking when they said to him, "Silver and gold have I none," meaning, "For a million dollars you won't get a new pair of legs, and what you need, my son, is legs. We understand your case—silver and gold won't give you legs, the real legs that you want." So Peter said, "Look on us," and when he looked on them, he said, "In the name of Jesus Christ of Nazareth rise up and walk," and he walked.

Now this lame man that was healed, didn't go to sleep after he was restored to health, but he followed them. Many of us, after we receive the salvation of Jesus, go to sleep spiritually. We go to church on Sunday morning, but we don't walk consistently with Jesus moment by moment. And that's the reason we have no testimony and no power; we're powerless Christians because WE JUST DON'T WALK WITH JESUS!

If you read in the Acts of the Apostles a little further, in chapter five, verse 15, you will see that a while after the healing of this beggar in the gate of the temple, the people brought their sick out into the streets and laid them on beds and couches, that the shadow of Peter passing by might fall on some of them, and they might get healing. From this illustration from the Scriptures, you can see how the Eastern mind works, can't you?

And the Eastern mind is the same now, and works the same now, as it did in the time of Abraham, as it did in the time of Jacob, as it did in the time of Jesus, and as it does in my time today. Our people are the same, and our thinking and our living is absolutely according to our religion. I can confirm these things to you, because I not only come from India, but I have traveled through these Bible lands, and I have checked on all these points. That is why I can tell you these facts so accurately and so fearlessly.

So I appeal to you to come over to the Eastern countries, and learn about these things, and then come back and teach your people. But generally it is the other way around. Instead of coming to learn something, you come over to teach us something. We in the East are glad when you come, but you must learn something, too, and so often, the Western people learn nothing at all. Instead of saying that you have come to teach the men who are the natives of India, you must come to learn something to take back and teach the natives in your own country. Many people do not like me, because I speak this way, but I am sent to speak this way, it is my work. The fact is, if you want to know the religious background of the Bible, you must come to the East to get it. Let us be humble and go to the right places to learn religion and philosophy.

Another place where the beggars go, who are seeking

healing for their incurable conditions, besides the high-way sides and the temple gates, is to the holy waters, generally holy rivers. Here, along the banks of the Ganges, the Euphrates, and the Tigris, hundreds of beggars line the banks, waiting for the troubling of the waters. For thousands of years, from generation to generation, the people of the East believe that one of the ways of getting healed is to wait on the banks of the holy rivers, and to get into that spot of water that is troubled. Very seldom does anyone ever get cured by this means, but it is all the hope that they have.

In this connection, in the fifth chapter of John, when Jesus went to the pool of Bethesda, there was a certain man lying there that had been there for 38 years, the Book says. He was waiting for a chance to get into the pool first after the waters were troubled, so that he might be healed. Can you wait 38 years for something from God? No, most of us ask today, and become discouraged if we do not have the thing we ask for by tomorrow. But this man had waited 38 long years! And the Bible says that Jesus knew how long he had waited; it says, "Jesus saw him lie, and knew that he had been now a long time in that case." Some of you say that you have been praying for your husband for 38 years. What is 38 years with God, when a thousand years is as one day with the Lord? Don't get impatient for anything; don't get in a hurry, because Jesus knows how long your heart has been desiring the things for which you have prayed.

Jesus asked the man, "Wilt thou be made whole?" The man answered Jesus, "Sir, I have no man, when the water is troubled, to put me into the pool: but while I am coming, another steppeth down before me." Instead of saying to Jesus, "Yes, I want to be made whole," this man brought his failures and faults to Jesus. Many of us, like this impotent man, bring our failures and our faults before Jesus. Don't crowd Jesus with your defeats, because your failure does not mean failure to God. Forget the past, and begin anew with Jesus. Cast out the old thoughts of defeatism, of fear, of dread and gloom, and put on the new man in Christ Jesus!

One of the Hindu teachings is that YOU control YOUR mind, and YOU control YOUR body, so that YOU can bring into captivity the flesh and the mind. Because YOU are the boss, YOU can tell the mind, "Mind, look here, you must think only this way, you must think only on Christ Jesus, and on no other thing." That is why the Hindus can kneel and pray for hours without their thoughts wandering, or without being upset over little things. You, too, can tell your mind that it must not think thoughts of fear, of doubt, of unbelief, of selfishness, of spite, of arrogance, of ignorance and of denominationalism, but put on the new man, with the mind of Christ, and think thoughts of love, of faith, of success, of victory and of joy! What a mighty teaching this is!

You do not have to cry to God like a parasite and say, "Lord, Lord, Lord, take me to heaven, Lord, because I am no good here." That sort of Christian is just a parasite! We are born to succeed here! We are made victorious here! We live eternal lives here! We are born to love here! We are more than conquerors through Jesus Christ here! We don't practice, neither do we demonstrate the power of Christ in us, and that's why we are full of fear and scared to death. That's why people do not come to Christ, because they see no demonstration of Christ in us!

So blind Bartimaeus sat at the highway side begging. When Jesus was passing by he cried, "Jesus, thou son of David, have mercy on me," and he would not cease crying out to Jesus, because he was there by the highway side for that very purpose. The Bible doesn't say how long he was there; he might have been there for 50 years, I don't know, but the lame man at the pool had been waiting there 38 years. I know people in India who have been waiting in one of these places 35 years, and have not been healed yet.

Jesus commanded him to be called. And he, casting away his robe, rose, and came to Jesus. Why "robe," instead of "garment"? Because the Jews in Palestine put on a robe to show their dignity, and their prestige. In India, the Hindus wear a turban on their heads for the same purpose, to show their caste, their dignity and their prestige. The Jews in Palestine do not wear a turban, but do wear a robe, and the longer the sleeves of the robe are, the greater the personage. If a big Sheik is walking, the sleeves will touch the ground, and the people will know because the sleeves are touching the ground that he is a most important person. The robe is white, and as he walks, the robe and sleeves sweep the floor.

When a man wants to fight anyone, or wants to declare war, or wants to defend anyone, he takes his robe off, puts the robe on his back, and ties the two sleeves around his neck in front. This leaves his arms bare, so that he can fight. In Isaiah 52:10, the Bible says, "The Lord hath made bare his holy arm in the eyes of all nations. . . ." "God hath made bare his holy arm" means that God is ready to heal, to save and to defend, all that call upon Him. He has put away His robe behind His back. His hands are strong; His hands are free to save all that come to Him, either for healing or for salvation. Do you see the Eastern picture?

Now the Jews wear this kind of a robe, and blind Bartimaeus had this kind of a robe. Even though he was blind, yet each day he would wear this robe while begging, so that people passing by would say, "Oh, look at that man. He's a good man, a cultured man, an educated

man, he is not a pauper. He is there just for healing."
That's what the robe tells in Palestine; that's what the
turban tells in India. We in the East, are judged by the
clothes we wear. Blind Bartimaeus wore the robe to
signify his position, his social standing, his dignity. But
when Jesus called him, he cast away his robe—Jesus
didn't tell him to cast away his robe, he did it without
being told. Jesus asked him, "What wilt thou that I
should do unto thee?" Bartimaeus said, "Lord, that I
might receive my sight."

How pleased Jesus must have been with this man,
because he cast away this robe of dignity and prestige!
This man ordinarily wore this robe to get the due and
proper respect of the passers by, and he wore it all the
time, but when he came to Jesus, he cast it off. Why?
He could have come to Jesus with his robe on and said,
"Lord, I'm a big sheik's son, you know. I never did
anyone any harm, Lord. I've always done that which is
right." People in this day do talk like that! They say that
they have kept the sermon on the mount, that they go to
church when they can, and that they have never harmed
anybody. In this country, the people even get angry when
you ask them, "Are you a Christian?" Their answer is,
"What do you think I am, a Chinese?"

Because THEY WERE BORN in America, most
people think that they are Christians. But this is not so;
rabbits are born in America, but they are not Christian,
are they? Of course not! A man is not a Christian
because he goes to church—a man is not a Christian
because he was born next door to a church—A MAN
IS A CHRISTIAN ONLY BECAUSE HE IS BORN
AGAIN! And "born again" means to accept Jesus Christ
individually and personally, and say in your heart, "Lord
Jesus, I'm a sinner, and you died for my sin. Come into
my heart and save me, Lord. Thank you." When you do

that, you will be saved and born again. In that moment that you believe, you will be born again. The Bible says, "Believe on the Lord Jesus Christ, and thou shalt be saved." (Acts 16:31). That is what being a Christian means. That is why I am a Christian, because I have done these things.

India had Christianity long before Europe had Christianity. But India doesn't claim to be a Christian nation. There are Christians in India, but India is not a Christian nation. India heard about Jesus Christ 60 years before Europe heard about Him, through Saint Thomas, the disciple of Jesus, but while India heard the Gospel story through him, they were not saved. Hearing about the Gospel and hearing about the Lord Jesus Christ is one thing; hearing about and accepting Jesus as Saviour is another thing! Plenty of Americans have heard about Jesus, but are not Christians. Why? Because they did not accept Jesus. You are not a Christian until you accept Jesus! That is what makes a man a Christian!

Blind as Bartimaeus was, he had a lot of good sense and wisdom! He must have thought to himself, "What is the good of my going to Jesus Christ, the King of Kings and Lord of Lords, with my own self-righteousness, with my own self-imposed dignity. These things are just filthy rags, before Jesus. I will cast off these dirty rags, and humbly go to Jesus." That which is righteousness to mankind, what seems good to our society, is just a dirty old rag before God. The Bible says, "But we are all as an unclean thing, and all our righteousnesses are as filthy rags. . . !" (Isaiah 64:6). This is so, because God looks not at the outward appearance, but at the heart. Do you see this point? And this man, Bartimaeus, believed in his heart that it was not good that he go before the King of Kings, the Saviour of mankind, all dressed up in the filthy rags of his own self importance and self righteousness! He believed in his heart that he would get a robe of righteousness from Jesus, as well as healing!

A person can't get mercy, and sympathy, and grace from Jesus when he's filled with self importance, self arrogance, self ignorance and self determination! You will have to throw out all that junk when you come to Him. A person has to say, "Lord, I have emptied myself, my heart, my mind, my all. I have put all my pride and superstition and ignorance in the rubbish bin. I come to thee, Lord Jesus, the fountain of living waters. Put all my self importance away, Lord, because it has only been a hindrance to me!" That's what blind Bartimaeus meant when he cast away his robe. Blessed Jesus, what a mighty man he was!

Every night, after these meetings, the Pastor asks you to come and be saved. Each night he asks you to come forward, and let us pray with you. How many come? Though I'm not a prophet, I can tell by the look of you, who is happy, content and joyful on the inside, because what is on the inside, will show on the outside. There are many people here who are full of self-importance, and self-righteousness, who are miserable, oppressed, laden with cares and burdens and troubles, yet you will not come to be saved. Why? It is because of fear—fear of what the people will say if you walk to the altar. Your mind tells you such things as "Look here, you are a deacon in your church, what would your minister say if you went forward here for salvation? What would my customers say? What would my neighbors say when they found out I had gone forward for salvation?" These are the fears that are keeping you away from Jesus, and away from the joy and peace of a man whose sins are forgiven. You listen to these silly ideas of your mind, and you are carried away from the Word of God!

But blind Bartimaeus was not carried away with any

silly ideas like this. He didn't care about his self-importance, he didn't care about his self-righteousness, he
didn't care a hoot about anything, except that here was
a man, Jesus of Nazareth, who could open his blind eyes.
He was going to meet a man who could do that which
this robe could not do. I will listen to Jesus, Bartimaeus
thought, rather than any old Tom, Dick or Harry, because Jesus can liberate me and set me free, and the
others can only hurl insults. The others can only frighten
us with their self-importance and self-righteousness, BUT
CHRIST CAN SET US FREE.

Then blind Bartimaeus came to Jesus, and my, Jesus
was pleased. "What wilt thou that I should do unto thee,
my son?"

"Lord, that I might receive my sight."

You threw that junk away, you're alright, you are pre-
pared; "Go thy way; thy faith hath made thee whole." It
was faith that made Bartimaeus throw away his self-
importance, his self-made righteousness, his love of self,
his fear of what people would say and his worry about
who would be looking at him. In America, people are
not ashamed of who sees them at a ball game, they are
not ashamed of themselves at a billiard table, but they are
ashamed to have anyone see them come to Jesus for
salvation. Oh, Jesus, have mercy on us tonight!

Won't you come to Jesus Christ tonight? It doesn't
cost you anything to come and you'll be richer because
of your coming. When the Hindus come to the Lord
Jesus Christ for salvation, it costs them a lot. They are
stripped of all their money, of all their position, of all
their lands and houses, of all their family, as you, who
have heard my story, know. You don't get these things
taken away from you, so what are you afraid of tonight?

Put out the old man of fear, and put on the new man
of faith, and come to Jesus. You can do it, because Jesus

will help you do it! Come walking down front here tonight, with the words of that great hymn on your lips, "Just as I am without one plea, but that Thy blood was shed for me, and that Thou bidd'st me come to Thee, O Lamb of God! I come, I come."

Bartimaeus received his sight, but he had to empty himself first. Shall we empty ourselves tonight of all the dirt and dust and self-imposed man-made fear, and come to Him tonight? You do not have to join this church here, you can go to your own church. I am preaching here, and I am an Eastern Orthodox Church Bishop, so what have you to be afraid of? Do you think I am afraid that my church will throw me out because I am preaching here? No sir! I was not afraid to give up my religion at so great a cost in order to come to Christianity. I fear God first, and no one else, because I do not have time to fear anybody!

Don't be afraid of any man. Get right with God, and get delivered from the inside. Throw away all the old junk first and then let Christ make you anew. Then you will have peace and gladness on the inside, and you will go home tonight a Lion of Judah, a son of God, a daughter of God. Then you will be able to throw your shoulders back and look up to Jesus and know that from hence forth, you don't belong to any religion, but you belong only to Christ, the Son of the living God!

May God bless you, goodnight.

www.ingramcontent.com/pod-product-compliance
Lightning Source LLC
Chambersburg PA
CBHW060652030426
42337CB00017B/2583